THE BEST OF TODAY'S DOGG

GUY GILCHRIST

PUBLISHED BY FASTPENCIL, INC.

Published by FastPencil, Inc.
3131 Bascom Ave.
Suite 150
Campbell CA 95008 USA
(408) 540-7571
(408) 540-7572 (Fax)
info@fastpencil.com
http://www.fastpencil.com

Today's Dogg is a trademark of Guy Gilchrist.

Follow Guy and Today's Dogg on Facebook and Twitter -
Twitter: @GuyGilchrist
On Facebook: Guy Gilchrist, Guy Gilchrist Fan Club, Today's Dog by Guy Gilchrist, Today's Dogg

FastPencil PREMIERE is an imprint of FastPencil, Inc.
For more information visit:
Premiere.fastpencil.com

This collection is dedicated to everyone who loves animals…..and inspired by those animals we love. There are millions of giving, amazing people who do so, so much for animal rescue and adoption, and all sorts of humane services. YOU are a constant inspiration to me, and a constant blessing to the animals you love so dearly. THANK YOU

᳚

"TODAY'S DOGG is dog-gone funny… no bones about it! I know you'll enjoy this bodacious collection from the mind and pen of one of the most talented and prolific cartoonists I know - Guy Gilchrist!"
- John Rose Cartoonist, King Features' Barney Google and Snuffy Smith comic strip

"TODAY'S DOGG not only tickles my funny bone, it caresses my heart. It reminds me of all the pets I've had in my life and recalls many fond memories."
- Mort Walker Creator of Beetle Bailey and Hi & Lois

"With TODAY'S DOGG, Guy has found his calling. He can relate so well with these trusting furry friends because he has the heart of a pet… trusting, honest, and nothing fake about him! With all of his diverse talents, I think his work on TODAY'S DOGG truly reflects his authentic caring nature."
- Marcus Hamilton Cartoonist for The Daily Dennis the Menace

᳚

CONTENTS

FOREWORD

or FURWORD…

All through my life, personally and professionally, I've been associated with children and animals. Children and animals are so honest. So loving. Nothing fake about them. That's why they have always owned my heart.

TODAY'S DOGG is about that honesty. It's the most fun I can have writing and drawing.

I love writing, whether it's a song, a book, a comic strip, or a poem. And no one ever gets to see it or hear it unless I know it's as honest and real as I can make it.

As soon as I started posting this cartoon on FaceBook, I got messages and emails online, and comments and stories on the streets of Nashville about it, and about peoples' dogs. All kinds of stories. Loving ones, funny ones, heartwarming ones….and troubling ones. I realized early on that this feature wasn't going to be like anything else I'd ever done. It really touched people. Not so much because of what I wrote or drew, but because people love their animals, and all animals, so, so deeply. I do , too. This cartoon was a real and honest connection between us.

Among our fans on FaceBook were hundreds of RESCUE and ADOPTION Groups, National, Regional and many of them GrassRoots. So it stood to reason I offered any help I could to those groups. That's how we came up with the idea of having an Outreach as part of Today's Dogg. A sizable portion of all profits we make on this feature and its' products go to helping these groups. This will continue to be as much a part of Today's Dogg as the writing and drawing… ….

and the slobbering, and the shedding….and the sniffing…..and the knocking over garbage cans…..and the begging at the table…..and the wetting…..and the petting… and the walking… ….and the unconditional loving.

Guy Gilchrist
August 2010
Nashville, TN

1

ABOUT THE AUTHOR

Guy Gilchrist has been in the business of being creative across all genres of art his entire life. He is an International, Multi-Award winning Writer of 48 Children's Books, Cartoonist of the comic strips "Nancy","Jim Henson's MUPPETS" and "Your Angels Speak,"a hit Nashville Songwriter, Recording Artist, and character designer for Tom & Jerry, Pink Panther, Looney Tunes & Disney, and Founder of an acclaimed Art School. And now: TODAY'S DOGG!!

Guy's work can be found everywhere, all over the world, as well as in the White House, where Guy was President Reagan's Guest of Honor in 1984, with art enshrined in The Smithsonian Institute, Washington, DC. Guy's Nancy Comic Strip, syndicated by United Feature Syndicate, runs in 350 newspapers, in 80 countries and on the web at www.comics.com and www.guygilchristmusic.com. Guy's Music can be found at his website (www.guycilchrist-music.com) and through ITunes.

A portion of all proceeds from "Today's Dogg™" are donated to various grass-roots animal rescue groups.

2

TODAY'S DOGG

TODAY'S DOGG™ By Guy Gilchrist

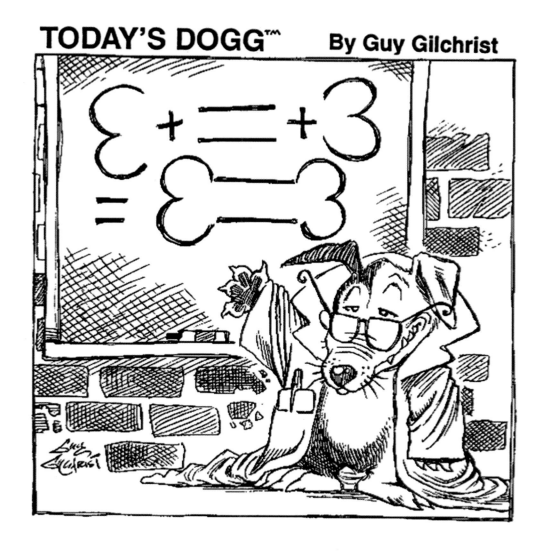

TODAY'S DOGG™ By Guy Gilchrist

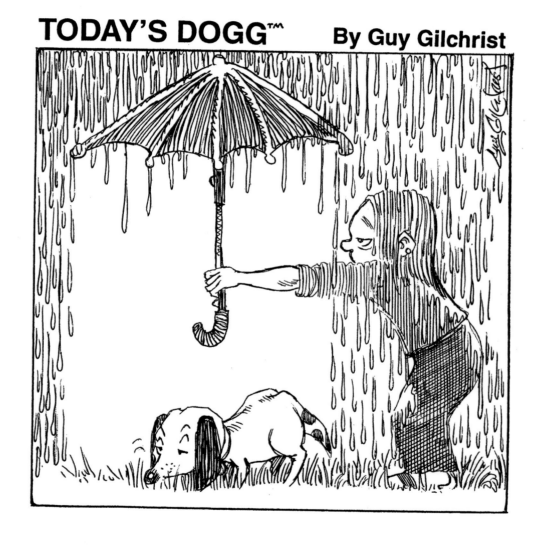

TODAY'S DOGG™ By Guy Gilchrist

TODAY'S DOGG™
By Guy Gilchrist
I KNOW, BUDDY,...ME, TOO! HANG ON TILL THE COM-MERCIAL! HE'S GOT A "NO-HITTER GOING!"
NHRA

TODAY'S DOGG™
By Guy Gilchrist
"BE STRONG AND COURAGEOUS. DO NOT BE AFRAID OR TERRIFIED BECAUSE OF THEM, FOR THE LORD, YOUR GOD GOES WITH YOU. HE WILL NEVER LEAVE OR FORSAKE YOU."
SO, THE BIBLE SAYS WE HAVE THE SAME DEAL WITH GOD THAT I HAVE WITH YOU GUYS!

TODAY'S DOGG™ By Guy Gilchrist
A DOGG™ FACT: AN OLD CHEW FOUND IN THE DIRT, WITH MOLD, AND BUGS, AND WHO-KNOWS-WHAT ELSE ON IT IS INFINITELY MORE APPEALING THAN THE NEW ONE YOU TRY TO BRIBE YOUR DOGG WITH, TO GET THE DISGUSTING ONE OUT OF THEIR MOUTH.
OOH.... LOOK... YUM!!

TODAY'S DOGG™
By Guy Gilchrist
INVITING THE NEW NEIGHBOR TO THE BIG WEEKEND B-B-Q...
THANKS, BUT I WON'T KNOW ANY-BODY!
C'MON! SNIFF A FEW TAILS, MARK YOUR SPOT... AND MINGLE.

TODAY'S DOGG™   By Guy Gilchrist

TODAY'S DOGG™
By Guy Gilchrist
OKAY... MARMADUKE, GOOD. GOOD. SNOOPY. EXCELLENT. FRED BASSET. NICE. GARFIELD?! GET THAT BAG OF LASAGNA OUT OF HERE!
DOGG NEWS
IT'S A DOGG'S WORLD
GUY GILCHRIST

TODAY'S DOGG™   By Guy Gilchrist

LAPTOP NO. 1

TODAY'S DOGG™
By Guy Gilchrist
TIME FOR YOUR WALK, BOY?
NO....IT'S TIME FOR MY "WALK, STOP, SNIFF, MARK, WALK IN CIRCLES, STOP, SMELL, BARK AT NOTHING, MARK, SMELL IT, RUN OFF WITH THE LEASH"! YOU KNOW... THE USUAL.

TODAY'S DOGG™ By Guy Gilchrist

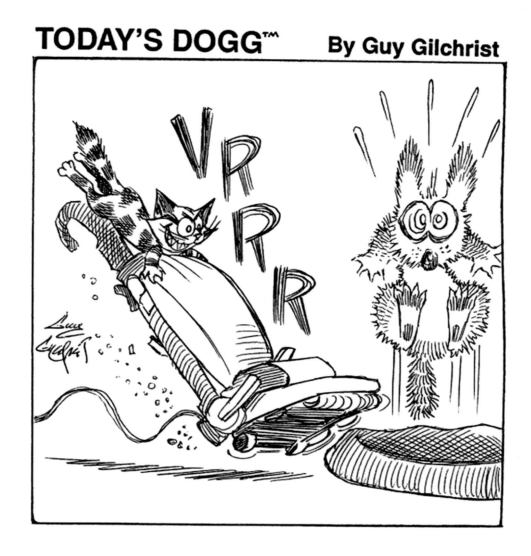

TODAY'S DOGG™   By Guy Gilchrist

I'LL JUST BURY IT HERE IN THE WRENCHES.

TODAY'S DOGG™   **By Guy Gilchrist**

"ASK THE BEER GIRL IF SHE HAS ANY MEAT."

TODAY'S DOGG™   By Guy Gilchrist

TODAY'S DOGG™   By Guy Gilchrist

FRIENDSHIP RING

TODAY'S DOGG™ By Guy Gilchrist

TODAY'S DOGG™ By Guy Gilchrist

TODAY'S DOGG™   **By Guy Gilchrist**

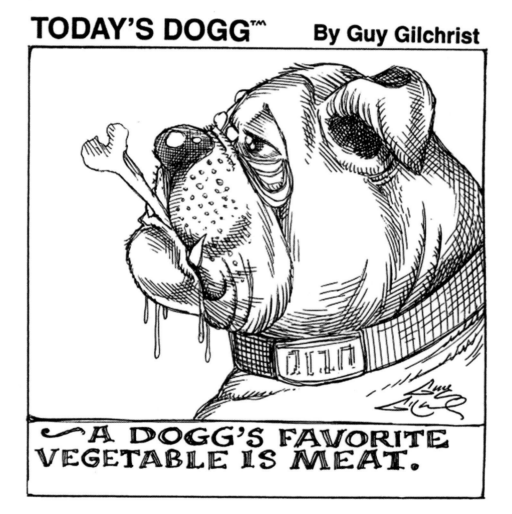

A DOGG'S FAVORITE VEGETABLE IS MEAT.

TODAY'S DOGG™
By Guy Gilchrist
OKAY. I'VE GOT HIS CREDIT CARD, THE PHONE, AND THE MENU! NOW...WHO CAN SPEAK "HUMAN" SO WE CAN ORDER THE PIZZAS?
Guy Gilchrist
PIZZA

TODAY'S DOGG™   By Guy Gilchrist

SCARY MOVIE NO. 1

TODAY'S DOGG™ By Guy Gilchrist

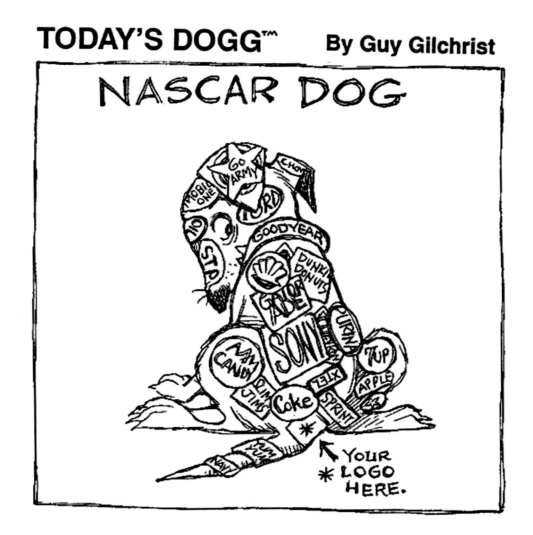

TODAY'S DOGG™ By Guy Gilchrist

LAPTOP NO. 2

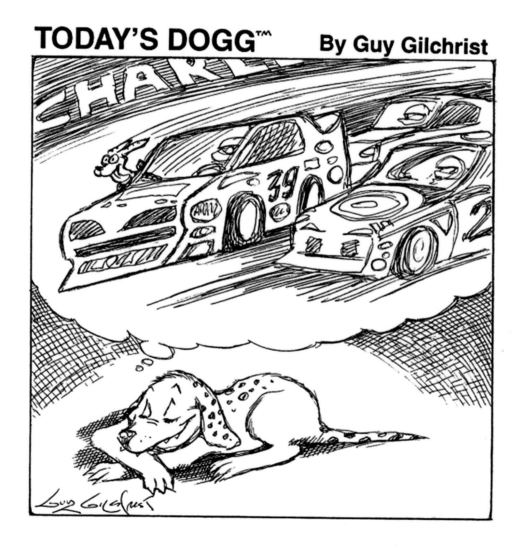

TODAY'S DOGG   By Guy Gilchrist

A BREAK FROM RACING

TODAY'S DOGG™ By Guy Gilchrist

TODAY'S DOGG™ By Guy Gilchrist

TODAY'S DOGG™   **By Guy Gilchrist**

TODAY'S DOGG™   By Guy Gilchrist

SCARY MOVIE NO. 2

TODAY'S DOGG™   By Guy Gilchrist

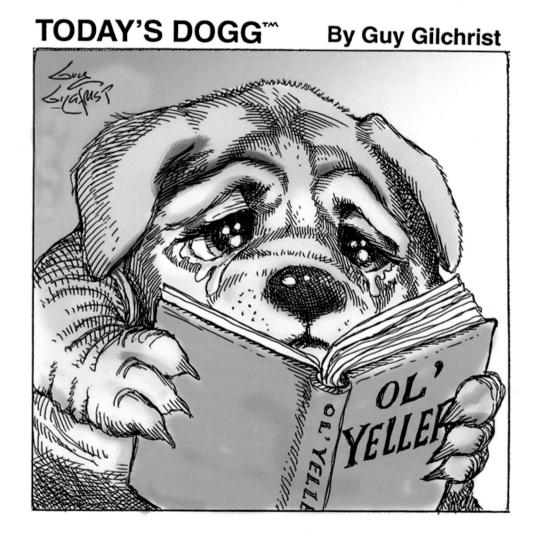

TODAY'S DOGG™ By Guy Gilchrist

TODAY'S DOGG™ By Guy Gilchrist

WHILE LOVE MIGHT BE COMPOSED OF A SINGLE SOUL INHABITING TWO BODIES, AS ARISTOTLE SAID... IT'S STILL BEST TO HAVE A COUPLE SEPARATE RAW-HIDE CHEWS.

TODAY'S DOGG™   By Guy Gilchrist

TODAY'S DOGG™   By Guy Gilchrist

STOWAWAY.

TODAY'S DOGG™ By Guy Gilchrist

TODAY'S DOGG™　　By Guy Gilchrist

TODAY'S DOGG™   By Guy Gilchrist

LAPTOP No. 3

TODAY'S DOGG™   By Guy Gilchrist

TODAY'S DOGG™ By Guy Gilchrist

TODAY'S DOGG™
By Guy Gilchrist
"YOU MUST BE FAMISHED. MAY I OFFER YOU A DRINK, MY DEAR?"

TODAY'S DOGG™   By Guy Gilchrist

SCARY MOVIE NO. 3

TODAY'S DOGG™ By Guy Gilchrist

TODAY'S DOGG **By Guy Gilchrist**

TODAY'S DOGG™
By Guy Gilchrist
DOGGS LOVE BASEBALL. ESPECIALLY WHEN ROLLED THROUGH BARBECUE SAUCE.

TODAY'S DOG   By Guy Gilchrist

TODAY'S DOGG™ By Guy Gilchrist
EVERYBODY'S GOIN' OUT AN' ♫ HAVIN' FUN! ♫ SNIFFIN' ROUND AND CHASIN' KITTIES IN THE SUN ♫ BUT, I'M IN HERE ♫ BECAUSE OF WHERE I PEED ♫ OH! LONESOME ME ♫
GUY GILCHRIST

TODAY'S DOGG   By Guy Gilchrist

"NAW. IT'S COOL. HE'S MY DESIGNATED DRIVER."

TODAY'S DOGG™ By Guy Gilchrist

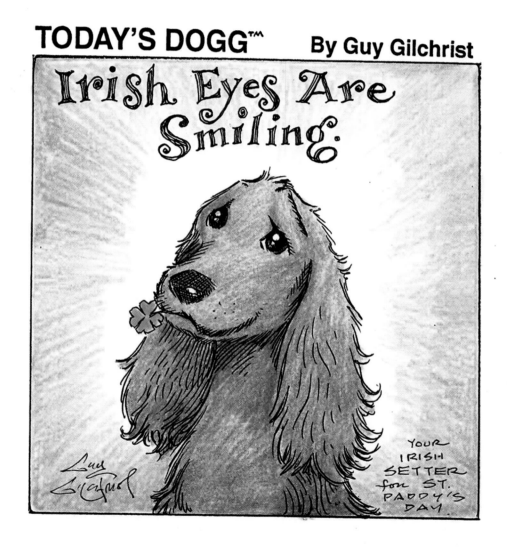

TODAY'S DOGG™   By Guy Gilchrist

3

TODAY'S DOGG TEAM

While I might write and draw the cartoons, this is not an individual's creation. Since the beginning, when I had the initial idea to do a panel about Dogs that would also have an animal outreach as part of the game plan, I have been blessed with these DOGG loving folks helping the dream along!

SHERRY ANDERSON

Sherry Anderson of Anderson Web Design, who maintains our website and takes care of so many fostered dogs as well as her own, I find it amazing she has time to have a meal, let alone build amazing websites.

LAURA TISDEL

Laura Tisdel, an amazing artist who adds the color to Today's Dogg, and loves our Boston Red Sox almost as much as she does animals.

JOHN AND DEBRA HNATH

To John and Debra Hnath, for their dedication to training and raising the most amazing tracking and search and rescue dogs....and the amazing photos John takes of those dogs, me, the world as he sees it.

BRUCE BUTTERFIELD

Bruce Butterfield, my Literary Agent, who believed in Today's Dogg the moment he saw it....and whose dachshund shows up in the cartoon all the time.

JAMIE JEAN

Jamie Jean of Train Productions, Nashville who makes all our Today's Dogg videos….as well as my music videos, and gives so much of himself to so many causes is a constant wonder to me. Oh…and thanks to Lewis, too…Jamie's Dogg, for letting me draw him.

MJ

MJ of PC Studios for putting all the cartoons together. The files on these cartoons were all over the place….and MJ just kept right on with the archaelogical dig until he unearthed them all!

MICHAEL ASHLEY

To Mash, at FastPencil…..for putting this all together.

AND OF COURSE…

Buddy, Sandy, Nitika, Heidi, Sollie, …and all the doggs of my life that will always be with me….in my drawings, and forever in my heart.